Modest!

General edition ISBN: 978-0-00-748755-4
Exclusive cover edition ISBN: 978-0-00-749982-3
1 3 5 7 9 10 8 6 4 2
First published in the UK by HarperCollins Children's Books in 2012

Studio photography by Simon Harris
Live photography by Chris Lopez, © Columbia Records
All other images used under licence from Shutterstock
Text by Jo Avery
Design by Wayne Redwood
Cover design by James Stevens
Production by Sian Smith

Printed and Bound in China

HarperCollins *Children's Books*

ONE DIRECTION

THE OFFICIAL ANNUAL 2013

ONE DIRECTION

CONTENTS

ONE DIRECTION

IT seems almost impossible now to think that there really was a time when no-one had heard of One Direction. Back in 2010, Harry Styles, Zayn Malik, Liam Payne, Niall Horan and Louis Tomlinson were devastated when they came third in The X Factor, behind Rebecca Ferguson and winner Matt Cardle. To the five hopefuls, it felt like their dreams were over before they'd even begun. If someone had told them that within a couple of years they would go from unknown singers to global superstars they would never have believed it. But that's exactly what happened. Ever since their stunning debut, *What Makes You Beautiful*, hit the top of the charts, One Direction's star has kept on rising. And it's still only the beginning...

- Their UK tour sold out in twelve minutes.
- Cumulatively, they have over 25 million followers on Twitter.
- Their global smash debut album, *Up All Night,* has sold over 3 million copies and reached number one in 16 countries. It has been certified triple platinum in Ireland, double platinum in the UK, three times platinum in Australia, double platinum in New Zealand and platinum in the US.
- Their debut album went to number one on the US Billboard chart. A first ever for a British band!
- They've played at venues across America, Australia and New Zealand on sell-out tours.

- They won a Brit Award for Best British Single.
- The *One Direction: Up All Night – The Live Tour* DVD has reached number one in 27 different countries worldwide, including the US, UK, Australia, France and Italy.
- They starred in Nickelodeon TV show *iCarly* in a special episode.
- They performed at the Nickelodeon Kids' Choice Awards in front of stars like Selena Gomez, Justin Bieber, Will Smith and the President's wife, Michelle Obama.
- Their video for *WMYB* has had over 170 million views.
- They are doing a massive world tour in 2013.

These five lads truly are taking the whole world by storm. And luckily, they want to share it all with you...

HARRY

I Heart Harry

DOB: 1st February 1994, making him the youngest member of 1D.

STAR SIGN: Aquarius.

HOME TOWN: The village of Holmes Chapel in Cheshire.

Harry's musical heroes are The Beatles and he's also a huge Coldplay fan.

His favourite TV show is *Family Guy*.

His fave movie is *Love Actually* – although he tells everyone it's *Fight Club* to seem more manly!

Harry's favourite song of all time is *Free Falling* by John Mayer.

He can play the kazoo.

He makes a brief cameo appearance in Ed Sheeran's unofficial video for his single, *Drunk*. It was filmed backstage at London Shepherd's Bush Empire.

When Harry was younger his hair was straight!

He doesn't like mayonnaise.

Harry has a sister called Gemma.

Before he took part in The X Factor, Harry had ambitions to be a lawyer.

Juggling is one of Harry's hidden talents.

What's the best thing about being in 1D?
"Being with four mates all of the time, going to cool places, meeting lots of nice people and having a laugh constantly. Even if we're really tired, we're still having a good time."

What's the secret of your success?
"I think people see us as down to earth. We don't try to act like big pop stars. We're attainable and we're friendly. None of us have changed, and I honestly don't think we will."

What's been your maddest celebrity moment?
"Probably meeting Michelle Obama. She was so nice and cool, and her kids were comfortable with talking to people they don't know. They were amazing. America was incredible in general. It's crazy to be recognised everywhere, but we loved it."

Do you have any other celebrity numbers on your mobile phone?
"I have some people I'm friends with, but if I say who they are I'll sound like I'm showing off! We've met a lot of people since we've been in the band, but we're still mates with all the people we were friends with before too."

STYLES

> **"I think people see us as down to earth. We don't try to act like big pop stars. We're attainable and we're friendly. None of us have changed, and I honestly don't think we will."**

When did you last cry? Why?

"It was on a plane when I was watching a film and I was so embarrassed I was trying to hide my face so no-one else could see me. I'm too ashamed to say what the film was because it shouldn't even have made me cry. It wasn't even that sad. I was just very tired and emotional because we'd been travelling for about 30 hours straight and I was a bit all over the place."

Do you have time for dating?

"I do, but it's hard because we're travelling so much. I guess you can always make time for things you want to do."

What are the most important qualities in a potential girlfriend?

"The most important thing for me is being able to get on with a girl easily. There's nothing better than being totally comfortable with someone and chatting for ages with no awkwardness. It's great when you can spend hours with someone and feel so content that you don't even have to talk that much if you don't want to. And a sense of humour is so important too. I like being able to laugh with someone and it's great when you find the same things funny and you get each other."

Where do you want to be five years from now?

"Doing exactly the same thing, please. I still want to be hanging out with the boys and travelling the world and having hits. I can't imagine anything I would rather do than this."

LIAM

I Heart Liam

DOB: 29th August 1993.

STAR SIGN: Virgo.

HOME TOWN: Wolverhampton.

Liam loves watching the *Toy Story* trilogy.

The movie *Marley & Me* made him cry. Bless.

He'd like to invent an anti-spoons app for mobile phones!

Liam is an avid fan of boxing.

He's also a West Bromwich Albion football fan.

His favourite song is *Happy Birthday* as it means he gets to open presents!

Liam would love to go into space!

He does a great Kermit the Frog impression!

Liam started crying during one of the band's acoustic performances of *More Than This*.

The desktop background on Liam's computer is of him with his family. When he misses them, the picture makes him smile.

When asked to describe him, the boys said Liam was, 'sensible, funny, daddy.'

What's the best thing about being in 1D?
"I get to travel the world with my four best friends, do brilliant shows, see the most amazing places and meet incredible people. We've been having such a laugh together and I think we got even closer with all the travelling and the craziness. We met Michelle Obama and you can't quite believe it when things like that happen. We showed her a picture of the statue of Barack Obama we bought Niall for his birthday and she loved it. We had to turn down an invite to the White House because we had shows booked in at the same time. How mad is that? It almost doesn't seem real."

What are you most proud of?
"I don't think it's anything we've won or achieved. I think it's the fact that we manage to make this job fun. We're five lads who were thrown together and we've managed to make it into a beautiful friendship while travelling around the world achieving brilliant things. Getting to number one in America was incredible, but it wouldn't mean as much if I wasn't with the lads."

Do you still get to do 'normal' stuff?
"We still do normal stuff all the time. Sometimes it's more difficult if you've got cameras around you, but whenever I check into a hotel I like to go out to the nearest shop and stock up on food and drinks so I don't have to rely on room service. I love doing that."

PAYNE

> ❝I get to travel the world with my four best friends, do brilliant shows, see the most amazing places and meet incredible people.❞

When you're on tour, what do you miss most about the UK?

"I miss my home town a lot. We were kind of pulled out of home after The X Factor and we didn't realise that we may not be going back. We've hardly been back at all and I do miss Wolverhampton. I really like going into the town centre and shopping and doing things like sitting on the sofa watching *Friends*. I'd even like to go back to school for a day. I hated it when I was there and I thought it was really hard work, but now I know what hard work is."

How do you come up with new songs?

"When I'm writing a song I usually think of songs I like at that time and write around them a bit. I don't know if that's cheating, but I do get inspired by other tracks. I think of the theme of a song and why I like it. I'll also grab a guitar and start plucking away and see what happens, or just sit at the piano and play. I write a lot of dance tunes on my iPad when I'm messing about and sometimes songs just happen."

If you could come back as someone else in your next life who would it be and why?

"I'd like to be a surfer. Since trying it in Australia I've fallen properly in love with it. Louis and I went loads and we're getting better all the time. We're still a bit messy around the edges, but it's so brilliant. I wish I'd tried it before. I could happily do it all day."

Do you Google yourself?

"Every so often if something interesting happens I'll have a look. After we'd been surfing I wanted to see pictures of us so I Googled them, but I don't read news articles and stuff. I try to stay away from them because you can get caught up in what other people think of you."

What qualities are important in a potential girlfriend?

"The first thing I look at are a girl's eyes. If someone has nice eyes and a nice smile that gets me interested. I also like someone I can have fun with. It's about having a good time with someone. I don't like people who are too in your face and it's important that someone knows you care about them and they don't need to worry about what's being said in the papers."

Where do you want to be five years from now?

"I'd like to be doing the same as we're doing now. What's happened to us is incredible and we could never have predicted it so why try and predict the future? As long as we work hard who knows where we'll end up?"

ZAYN

I Heart Zayn

DOB: 12th January 1993.

STAR SIGN: Capricorn.

HOME TOWN: Bradford, West Yorkshire.

Zayn has a soft spot for intelligent girls.

He can't swim.

'NSYNC is his favourite band of all time.

He supports Manchester United.

Doniya, Waliyha and Safaa are the names of Zayn's three sisters.

Until he was in One Direction, Zayn didn't have a passport.

His favourite song is *Thriller* by Michael Jackson.

He reckons he used to be a bit of a geek when he was younger and liked to collect comics.

Whenever the boys are mobbed, Zayn always looks out for Niall because he knows he gets claustrophobic.

One fan fainted while holding Zayn's hand!

Zayn's X Factor audition wasn't broadcast on the main show. It was shown later on the spin-off show, The Xtra Factor.

What's the best thing about being in 1D?

"The other four lads. I've got four very good mates out of being in the band and that's cool. We all keep each other down to earth and there's defo no way I could have done this as a solo artist. I would have cracked up and given it all up and gone home by now. The lads keep me grounded and it's good to know you're not the only person going through everything. We're sharing every experience."

Do your mates back home still treat you in the same way?

"Yes, and thank goodness for that. It's a massive help. I grew up with two close friends, Anthony and Danny, and they're like my brothers. They treat me completely normally and just like they did before. If I'm being an idiot they'll tell me and it's nice to have that because new people can often be a bit wary of us. My friends don't care that I'm in a band, I'm just a mate."

Tell us a secret!

"I'm double-jointed in my thumb. I can pop the bone in and out. I used to do it in front of my sisters when we were younger to freak them out."

What's the most extravagant thing you've bought?

"I'm not much of an extravagant spender. I've got pretty simple tastes and if anything I probably spend too much money on junk food like chocolate and sweets. The thing that's probably the most unjustifiable in terms of money is a Gucci bag that I bought. I had a bit of a thing for Gucci and for a while I always used to buy things when we went through airports. They cost a fortune!"

MALIK

What makes you happiest?

"When I'm home doing the most normal things. If I could go home tomorrow, I'd wake up late afternoon, come downstairs, sit on my sofa and watch TV and hang out with my family. I'd also take my sisters out shopping because I love seeing their reactions when I buy them stuff. I love seeing them happy."

What do you still want to achieve?

"So much. I still want to get a house for my parents and it's in the pipeline at the moment, which I'm massively excited about. I want to see how far we can take One Direction and hopefully down the line we'll get new fans who will like us because they realise that we're a good vocal group and they like our music. Even if we only convert a handful of people who weren't fans before and never expected to be, I'll be happy."

What's been your most embarrassing moment?

"Anything that involves dancing. Anything dance-related is awful for me. I don't take myself as seriously any more when it comes to dancing, but I still hate it as much as I always did."

On a scale of one to ten, how vain are you?

"I get the brunt of mickey-taking when it comes to being vain. I get made out to be the worst member of the group, but the truth is we're in a boy band so you have to be a little bit vain to keep yourself looking smart. Maybe I look in the mirror a bit too frequently, but that's because I care what I look like. But I really don't think I'm massively vain. I'm probably around a six or seven vanity-wise."

Where do you want to be five years from now?

"I'd like One Direction to still be going and I'd like our fan base to have grown. I'd also like my own house and I'll possibly be settling down and looking to get married."

What qualities are important in a potential girlfriend?

"Someone who's chilled out and doesn't take themselves too seriously, and who wouldn't have a hissy fit over little things. I like girls who enjoy simple things. I want someone I can sit on a sofa with for hours and hours, just chatting away. I used to think I liked a specific look and that was girls with dark hair and coloured eyes, but that's not the case any more because I find all sorts of girls attractive. Obviously you've got to be attracted to someone to be in a relationship, but at the same time it's not a massive deal. Someone who looks after themselves and has a bit of confidence is attractive, but we've got to be friends as well."

> **" I've got four very good mates out of being in the band and that's cool. "**

LOUIS

I Heart Louis

DOB: 24th December 1991.
He's the oldest member of One Direction.

STAR SIGN: Capricorn.

HOME TOWN: Doncaster,
South Yorkshire.

Louis reckons the band always eat Haribo sweets before gigs. "We do the sweets like they're drinks. We 'cheers' them. It's very strange, but it's for good luck."

Look After You by The Fray is his favourite song.

Louis's first word was 'cat'.

Louis and Harry are the only members of 1D so far who have passed their driving tests.

If Louis had a superpower, he would fly.

The rest of the band all thought Louis was quiet when they first met.

He absolutely hates to be tickled.

Talking too much is Louis's worst habit!

He reckons chilli-flavoured ice cream is AMAZING!

What's the best thing about being in 1D?

"Pretty much everything. We never expected to release in America and get the kind of reaction we did, so that's been amazing. And to then go on and do so well in Australia was incredible. It's great to visit so many different places and I love performing on stage to thousands of people and seeing the audience waving banners and wearing One Direction T-shirts. And we're still having such a good time as mates, which is the main thing."

How are you handling life as an international pop star?

"I don't know if I would consider myself an international pop star! It seems crazy to put that title on us. I still think of myself as a normal guy. I just keep in contact with everyone from back home and have as much fun as I can. We all laugh constantly. I honestly don't think I'd be able to hack being a singer if I was doing this on my own. We keep each other sane."

Who's surprised you by being one of your fans?

"I thought it was pretty sick that Katy Perry was dancing along when we performed at the Kids' Choice Awards in America. I really like her, so that was pretty cool."

TOMLINSON

> ## " We're a bit rebellious and don't do everything we're told to and we've got our own minds. "

If you could have anyone round for dinner, who would it be?

"I'd have an ancient Egyptian round because that sort of stuff fascinates me. I'd ask them how they built the pyramids and find out about their rituals and how they discovered medicines. I'd love to learn all about it."

Describe your perfect day.

"I'd like to go back home and do the kind of things I used to do before the band. I'd go and have a kick around with my friend Stan and my other friends from school. I'd spend some time with my family and have dinner at my grandma's house and then have the evening to chill out with my girlfriend."

Who would play you in the movie of your life?

"I love Jim Carrey, but I don't think I look very much like him... I'll say Leonardo DiCaprio because he's a brilliant actor and someone said to me I look like him in the film *Titanic*, which I was very pleased about."

Why do your fans connect with you so much?

"I think we're just people who you can relate to. We haven't come from stage school and trained and everything. We're five guys who do what we do and we haven't changed. We're a bit rebellious and don't do everything we're told to and we've got our own minds. We're real and we're not trying to be untouchable."

What qualities are most important in a potential girlfriend?

"Someone who doesn't take life too seriously and likes to take a risk. I like to do things on the spur of the moment. I decided to go to Ibiza for one night recently so I jumped on a plane and my girlfriend came with me. I love that 'let's just do it' attitude. It's also important that someone totally trusts you and is your friend above everything else. They've also got to have a good sense of humour because the only way I can pull girls is by making them laugh."

EXCLUSIVE INTERVIEW

NIALL

I Heart Niall

DOB: 13th September 1993.

STAR SIGN: Virgo

HOME TOWN: Mullingar in Ireland.

Niall's favourite movie of all time is *Grease*.

He's left-handed.

His favourite colour is blue.

Niall's good luck mascot is a pair of white socks.

He has an older brother called Greg.

When Niall's mum visited him in the US he wouldn't let her pay for anything!

Playing the guitar is one of Niall's many talents.

He's learning how to dive.

Niall is the only member of 1D who wasn't born in the UK.

He has a soft spot for girls with green eyes.

What's the best thing about being in 1D?
"The craic that we have together and with all the crew around us. It's a good laugh and when you're doing crazy hours and you're tired sometimes, you know the other lads are there for you. We also get to travel the world and we've got so many dedicated fans out there and that makes me smile every day."

Is fame how you imagined it?
"Yes and no. It's much harder work than it's made out to be. It looks like it's all glitz and glamour, but there are a lot of flights and interviews and photo shoots. A shoot can take hours and then only one picture will be used. Not that I'm complaining at all because I love it all, but it's not really what I expected it to be in some ways."

What's on your iPod?
"I've been listening to Olly Murs' album a lot and also James Morrison's newest one. I also love Noel Gallagher's High Flying Birds. Oh, and The Eagles. I've always been an Eagles fan. They used to come to Ireland every year and my dad and I always used to go and see them together so I've liked them from a young age."

HORAN

> " **I'd love to be doing a big world tour and still making great music.** "

What's the strangest rumour you've heard about yourself?

"I once heard that we all died in a car crash on the way to our hotel after filming the *It's Gotta Be You* video. There was also a rumour that I was going out with Gillian McKeith's daughter. I only met her once backstage at The X Factor during rehearsals. Me and Gillian's daughter were stood next to each other and someone cropped the photo so it looked like we were the only two people in it. The other good rumour is that I had a fight with Justin Bieber because he thought I was hitting on his girlfriend, Selena Gomez. I'd never even met her!"

What's the one thing you can't live without?

"Apart from my heart, for obvious reasons, food. Not just because I need it to survive, but because I love it. I love Nando's and anything noodle-based, so I really like Wagamama."

What was your most recent dream?

"I dreamt that we were in a casino and stayed there all night hanging out with Brian McFadden. Brian and I split some chips and won a million Australian dollars. If only it was real."

Who's your celeb crush?

"Demi Lovato. She's absolutely stunning. I saw her at a Big Time Rush movie premiere and she's absolutely beautiful. I didn't speak to her, but I would like to."

Where would you like to be five years from now?

"I'd love to be doing a big world tour and still making great music. I want to have the same amazing fan base we've got. Who would ever think all of this would happen to us? So it's exciting to think what can happen in five years."

What are the most important qualities in a potential girlfriend?

"A good sense of humour, nice eyes, someone who isn't too clingy and someone who's carefree, like me. I like someone who likes to have a laugh basically. I like girlie girls but I'd also like someone who would come and watch football with me. It's also very hot if a girl can play an instrument."

BREAKING RECORDS

There's no doubt about it, One Direction are truly international pop stars...

To say One Direction are the hottest band on the planet right now doesn't quite grasp the situation. The band are taking the whole world by storm, scorching sales charts and box offices around the world. The five lads have seemingly done the impossible; no wonder hysteria has followed them right across the globe. They conquered the US, becoming the first UK group to see their debut album enter at No 1 on the Billboard chart – not even The Beatles managed that! And from the minute they arrived in America, Australia and New Zealand, they had to be escorted by security guards due to the number of fans desperate to see the band. Hordes of fans turned up at every single appearance the lads made, with messages written on boards, hoping to catch a glimpse of their idols.

"It just shows how incredibly dedicated our fans are and it's just amazing for us, you know, we're doing something that we love and to be appreciated for that is amazing," says Louis.

There's no doubt about it, One Direction are big news. You can hardly turn on a radio or TV without hearing their music or the boys themselves being interviewed. It has never happened like this before and never to a UK pop band. One Direction have achieved worldwide recognition, something few artists ever manage to do. They're breaking records and creating new ones almost as fast as anyone can stop and write them down.

Such is the boys' success that One Direction are being compared to super groups like The Beatles and the Rolling Stones, but the boys are taking all the hype with their customary good grace. "When people say that to us we kind of brush it off, because it seems like such a wild statement to be compared to The Beatles," says Niall.

And it seems like celebrities can't get enough of the boys either. When the band made an appearance in the US, Selena Gomez immediately took to her feet, dancing along with Taylor Swift and Ashley Tisdale. Even the President's wife, Michelle Obama, couldn't stop herself from clapping along too.

It would be incredibly easy for so much success gained so quickly to have gone to their heads. But of course that hasn't happened. Harry, Niall, Liam, Louis and Zayn are way too down to earth to let egos get in the way. "We don't have the time!" laughs Niall. Life has been a dizzying blur of travel, concerts, video shoots, interviews and TV appearances. "It's been insane," remembers Harry. "We're just riding the wave, working hard and having a lot of fun."

And the boys also know just how much they owe their success to their ever-growing army of fans. "If you ask our fans where they found out about us, it's always Twitter, YouTube, Facebook and Tumblr," says Niall. "Our fans have really got our name out there. We can't thank them enough!"

WE LOVE, LOVE, LOVE OUR FANS!

If there's one thing you can be sure of, it's that One Direction love you lot – their fans! They know that they wouldn't be where they are today without your support and devotion and they're super-keen that you know it.

Around the world

There are now Directioners all over the planet and the boys are recognised and adored almost everywhere they go.

When they started out, the band were hoping they'd be successful in the UK, but their success around the world has been beyond their wildest dreams. They remember arriving in France and getting swept away by the support – literally. By the time they got to the end of the train station they weren't walking any more, but were being carried along by a crowd of people. It was so crazy that Liam even lost a shoe!

People from around the world are going to gigs and meeting up with other fans that they've made friends with online. It's one big community – and the boys love it. As Liam says, "it's really cute that fans are making friends because of us."

The band are bowled over by the adoration of their fans. Niall remarks, "I doubt we'll ever get used to the screaming, you know. Even though it's everywhere we go! We can't believe it!"

Devoted fans

Some fans will go to great lengths to meet their idols. One fan flew from Australia to America on her birthday to meet the band at the airport – now that's devotion. Fans have also rushed up to the boys in the street and kissed them. That's something that doesn't happen to everyone. "We'd get slapped around the face if we did it," laughs Niall.

Carrots and more carrots

To be a little quirky, Louis said that he likes girls who eat carrots. Ever since, he's had lots of carrots sent and given to him by fans. The rest of the band joke that that's why Louis is tanned, and also why he's so good at seeing in the dark!

The band were also given other presents after Louis told a joke: 'Why did the mushroom go to a party? Because he's a fungi!' They were given a box of mushrooms with their faces drawn on. And Liam jokes that he doesn't even like mushrooms!

The boys know that without the Directioners they wouldn't be where they are today...

Likes and dislikes

Zayn, Liam, Louis, Niall and Harry have said that they love being given gifts and don't mind soft things, like teddy bears, being thrown. However, they don't like it when fans throw hard stuff, like carrots, or when their hair is pulled or their bums are squidged! So take note!

Their US fans

The boys are overwhelmed by the devotion of their fans all over the world – and are blown away by the support from America.

Liam says it's exciting that there are so many fans waiting outside hotels and venues. In Boston, the band did a meet and greet and five girls arrived, each dressed as

a member of 1D. "That was cool," says Harry. And when the boys are on the tour bus fans start climbing all over it, chasing it and banging on the windows, trying to get in.

Recognition

There are lots of devoted fans of the band and Liam, Niall, Harry, Zayn and Louis often recognise the same girls at gigs and other venues. The band's support is growing so quickly, though, that they say they've seen lots of new faces recently!

Liam says, "It's lovely to come out of your

hotel and see familiar faces. It's great." Louis also feels that it's good to know fans' names and to get to know them as people, "they become like our friends," he says.

What 1D love about the Directioners

Liam reports that the fans are amazing, "they know everything. They know our flight times, what gate number we are, where we're going... our fans are impressive!"

Louis says that 1D's fans are the best in the world and are so supportive.

Niall also thinks that they have the best fans on the planet. "We love and appreciate you, never think any other way. We love you so much!"

Winning the Brit Award was a highlight for Harry. He says it just blew the band away and winning was all down to the amazing fans. He'd like to say thank you to all of you.

Finally, Zayn says, "a massive thank you to all our fans. We love you all."

You know One Direction love their fans because...

 They buy them pizza.

 They worry about their fans getting soaked in the rain whilst waiting for them.

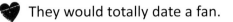 They always thank their fans and tell them they're amazing.

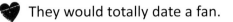 They would totally date a fan.

WHAT KIND OF DIRECTIONER ARE YOU?

Take our quiz to find out what kind of Directioner you really are.

1) The boys are heading off to Europe to shoot a video. Do you:

a) head to the airport and wait at the gate to wave them off?

b) have it down in your diary so you know where they are that day?

c) read about it on One Direction's official website?

d) find out through some mates at school?

2) You see One Direction walking down the street. Do you:

a) run at the boys screaming your head off, then burst into tears?

b) get all giddy, jump up and down, ask them to sign your bag and tell them how much you love them?

c) approach the boys and ask politely if you can have a picture?

d) nudge your mate and say, "Is that One Direction?" as you watch them walk by?

3) It's Louis's birthday. Do you:

a) bake and decorate a three-tier cake for him?

b) send him a card and some carrots?

c) tweet him happy birthday?

d) think, "Aah, that's nice, he's a Capricorn."?

4) Tickets for the tour are going on sale at 9am. Do you:

a) get your mum, dad, sister, aunt, nan and best mate to all start calling from 8.55am?

b) set your alarm to wake you up so you can start calling on repeat from 9am until you get through?

c) suddenly remember at 9.15am, get online and keep your fingers crossed that there are some left?

d) hope you win some in a radio competition?

5) The boys are coming to do a performance at your school. Do you:

a) give the boys the fan book that you've spent 135 hours on plus a print out of your fan fiction?

b) write the boys' names all over your school shirt and cheeks?

c) make sure you look your best, wear your 1D tee, and get a banner ready?

d) dig out your autograph book and take your camera so you can get some pics?

6) The boys spot you waiting outside a TV studio. Do they:

a) say hello and know your name?

b) come over, say, "Hi, you look familiar..."?

c) come over and have their picture taken with you?

d) not even notice you're a fan?

MOSTLY A)S
You are a very dedicated Directioner. There aren't many out there as loyal and devoted as you. The boys totes appreciate your huge devotion, but be careful you're not missing out on other important things.

MOSTLY B)S
You are a super-fan with posters all over your bedroom walls and you know loads about them. The guys wouldn't be where they are today without people like you! Enjoy, but don't forget your 'real-life' friends too!

MOSTLY C)S
You love Harry, Niall, Zayn, Louis and Liam and have posters of the boys all over your walls and follow the lads on Twitter, but you also make sure that you always have time for plenty of other things in your life too.

MOSTLY D)S
Hmm, are you sure you meant to pick up this book? Make sure you read it cover to cover and brush up on your 1D knowledge. With a little bit of time and dedication you will become a devoted Directioner.

LIFE ON THE ROAD

The boys have done more than their fair share of touring recently, wowing fans all over the world. So what's life like on the road? The boys reveal all...

THE SHOW

NIALL: "We sit down with a producer and go through the theme for it, and what happens with each song. It's just amazing and incredible."

HARRY: "We do everything we can to make sure everyone enjoys the show."

LIAM: "We're all really happy with it and hope you are too."

NIALL: "*Up All Night* is our favourite song to perform."

THE BANNERS

LOUIS: "It's amazing to see people in the crowd with a banner. I always look for really random ones."

NIALL: "Love them! They're brilliant! They're a good way of getting our attention 'cause we like to be able to see what the fans are doing during the concert. It's always good to read them because people put a lot of time into them!"

LIAM: "They can be really funny. Hilarious."

HARRY: "The crowds have been absolutely amazing."

ONE DIRECTION
10 &

THE TOUR BUS

ZAYN: "We've got our own tour bus. There's a Nintendo DS and we've got a console on there so we keep ourselves entertained. We're together all the time and there isn't one really annoying person, we're all just as annoying as each other."

NIALL: "The tour bus rules are that I get to sleep in the top bunk and that I can go to sleep whenever I want to. And I get to eat a lot."

LOUIS: "As long as I've got a comfy bed, I'm not really bothered. And loads of good music and films."

THE FOOD

LOUIS: "Our diets are not great – we often go for the fast food option."

NIALL: "If there's catering then I'm happy. I love eating!"

IT'S A SELL-OUT

ZAYN: "I'm massively proud. It's just crazy to think, 'Why would all these people come and see me?' It's really cool."

HARRY: "It's a very nice feeling that people want to come and see you."

ON TRAVELLING

ZAYN: "I'd never even seen a plane before I joined One Direction, so to be touring around and seeing lots of different countries, it's amazing."

HARRY: "We just want to work and try our best. The only thing I'd change about my life right now is that I'd like to see more of my friends and family."

ONE DIRECTION'S RIDER

HARRY: "People put stuff in our room, but we don't go there and tell them what we need. Basically, if you can get a cup of tea or a bottle of water it's fine."

LIAM: "We get sweets just because we're kids."

MISCHIEF ON TOUR

HARRY: "We've all just been having a lot of fun in the dressing rooms, getting up to mischief. Liam was asleep and Zayn shaved a slit in his eyebrow and then Zayn was asleep and I shaved my initials into his leg hair."

ONE DIRECTION

TOUR TRIVIA

- The boys like to skate around venues during their downtime, causing mischief.

- In their free time they like to play football and video games.

- One of their favourite stops on the One Direction tour was Wolverhampton because the boys had a hot tub and sauna in their dressing room! "That's it. Before every gig we are having a sauna or a bath together!" laughs Louis.

F@MOUS F@NS

It's not just Directioners who love Harry, Zayn, Liam, Louis and Niall. They have their fair share of celebrity fans too.

JLS WERE THE FIRST TO TWEET THEIR SUPPORT WHEN THE BOYS HIT THE NUMBER ONE SPOT IN AMERICA.
"Congrats to One Direction on their US no1 album! That's HUGE boys well done! Marv and the lads."

THEIR FAVOURITE FOOD GUYS-NANDO'S.
"You've got to give it to One Direction for getting a number one album in the US. Nice one lads, you've got some top fans out there."

CHERYL COLE DIDN'T WANT THEM TO FORGET HOW MUCH SHE'D HELPED THEM ON THEIR X FACTOR JOURNEY.
"Congratulations! @louis_tomlinson @niallofficial @harry_styles @zaynmalik @real_liam_payne remember who really mentored you when @simoncowell wasn't there LMAO!! #proudofyouboys"

OLLY MURS WAS QUICK TO SHOW HIS SUPPORT.
"WELL DONEEEEE!! One Direction #1 with Debut Album in US Billboard Charts!! 1st Ever UK Band to do it!! That's amazing stuff lads!! Ledge!!"

MEGA POPSTAR **KATY PERRY** IS ONE OF THEIR BIGGEST FANS. THE POP QUEEN PUT NIALL THROUGH DURING THE 2010 SEASON OF THE X FACTOR AND TWEETED HIM WHEN THE BAND HIT THE NO 1 SPOT.
"@NiallOfficial congratulations, you didn't let me down! xo"

LILY ALLEN IS A FAN TOO.
"It's amazing how well One Direction are being received across the pond, no? Good luck to 'em I say, seem like good lads."

FORMER BEATLE **SIR PAUL MCCARTNEY** HAS ALSO SAID ABOUT THE BOYS:
"Let's just call them the next terrific band. Doing well in America - good luck lads."

AND THE BIG MAN HIMSELF... SIMON COWELL.
"I couldn't be happier for One Direction. It is an incredible achievement. They deserve it. They have the best fans in the world."

HOME IS WHERE THE HEART IS ♥

When the boys have some rare time off, they like to kick back and chill out...

Relaxing at home

Any chance they get, the 1D boys all love to go home, see family and friends and recharge their batteries with some time away from the spotlight. Of his home, Liam remarks that he loves to spend time "in my bedroom, although I do quite like sitting in our kitchen. It's spacious with a great view."

Days off

On their rare days off, the band members have different ways of spending their time – some like to chill out while others love to stay active or party.

Niall feels that he has to be active – he likes to go to the shops or do something constructive with his days.

Zayn is the opposite and loves to chill; his ideal day off would involve waking at 5pm, relaxing at home, playing a few video games, watching a film, having a great meal and then going back to sleep again. Very relaxing!

Louis loves to party. He knows he should chill out on his rare days off, but he hates sitting around. "Every time I am back home I always make sure I see all my mates. I like to go out and party," he says. Like Liam, Harry also loves to party, although both of them also take time out to relax and spend quality time with their families.

Liam finds that he likes to have something to do all the time because he's so used to being busy.

Comfy clothes

Zayn, Niall, Liam, Louis and Harry have great fashion sense and even when relaxing at home they all have their own style.

Zayn loves to wear comfortable clothes – joggers and a really baggy T-shirt. He'll also put on a pair of high tops. Even on his days off he takes care of his grooming: "I'll still have a shower, do my hair, all the normal stuff. It's not the same grooming as for TV or anything, but I do like to look after myself."

Harry loves to pull on shorts and a T-shirt on his days off. He knows how to relax!

Louis has the strangest claim of all. He says that his house has lots of stairs, so if no-one is in, he'll run up them naked!

STYLE FILE

No-one does style like One Direction. The boys are masters at combining everyone's individual fashion sense while looking like a band.

Fashion Facts

1D own over 100 pairs of shoes between them.

Harry likes to look like a gentleman, with a hanky in the top pocket of his suit jacket. Very dapper.

At the Nickelodeon Kids' Choice Awards the boys all put their stamp on the monochrome black and white look. Harry with his blazer, Louis and his braces, Liam and his checked shirt, Zayn wearing a varsity jacket and Niall in a black collared T-shirt.

Harry was spotted taking fashion very seriously at London's Fashion Week.

⚡ 1D ZAYN ★

MOST LIKELY TO BE WEARING: Zayn's trademark look is a cool baseball-type jacket or cosy slim-fitting jumper, sloppy trousers and high top trainers. He will occasionally be seen wearing very geek-chic glasses. When he's smart, the formal checked shirts make an appearance with a blazer or a well-cut suit with industrial boots. On bad hair days, Zayn likes to wear a beanie hat.

HAIR: A cute perfectly styled quiff. He's always been passionate about his hair. "I was about 12 or 13 when I started taking pride in my appearance. I even used to get up half an hour earlier than my sister so I could do my hair. I had a few dodgy haircuts over the years. I shaved my head a few times and also had slits in my eyebrows."

ZAYN ON HIS STYLE:

"I like urban, more street – Nike trainers and varsity jackets."

 # HARRY

MOST LIKELY TO BE WEARING: Harry is possibly the only boy in the world who can pull off a bow tie with a tux without looking like a grandpa. He's partial to a blazer worn with jeans, chinos or as part of a suit. On his feet he likes Converse white pumps or various coloured suede desert boots. When he's dressing down he will often be seen hanging out in a Jack Wills hoodie.

HAIR: His trademark curly mop. He hates it if it gets cut too short.

HARRY ON HIS STYLE:

"I used to wear my jeans low; now I wear them high. I like my hair looking like I've just got out of bed."

NIALL

MOST LIKELY TO BE WEARING: Often seen in polo shirts and cardigans, Niall is the most casual in the band. On his feet, he sports Supra trainers, or retro Nike Dunks. When he's getting suited and booted, Niall goes for the skinny suits and often teams them with high top trainers to keep it casual.

HAIR: Various shades of blond. His favourite being what he calls Eminem blond. Sometimes quiffed, sometimes brushed forward, Niall's hair always looks cool.

NIALL ON HIS STYLE:

"My favourite shops are Top Man and Jack Wills. They're literally the only two shops I buy anything in at the moment."

LOUIS

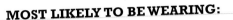

MOST LIKELY TO BE WEARING:

He loves a Breton striped top, either navy blue or red, with coloured jeans or chinos rolled up. On his feet will be his favourite VANS shoes or espadrilles when he's working a more casual look. For a smart look, Louis rocks a white shirt, tight trousers and his favourite accessory – braces. Oh, and let's not forget Louis's beloved one-piece!

HAIR: Louis likes to keep his style casual and his hair always looks great!

LOUIS ON HIS STYLE:

"Whenever I go on a flight I've always got my one-piece on. I can get on the plane, like long trips to LA, and just zip it right up. Just leave a hole at the top to breathe and go to sleep. It's amazing."

LIAM

MOST LIKELY TO BE WEARING: For rehearsals or hanging out, Liam can often be seen in a Superdry lumberjack shirt, with baggy jeans and high tops. He's also partial to a Superman T-shirt. When he's dressing up for a do, he mixes a smart suit with a tight waistcoat.

HAIR: Liam is the most likely to chop and change his locks. He started out with a swept-over fringe before chucking away his pink straighteners and going for a curly mop like Harry. Now it's shorter again. Luckily, it always looks great whether it's short, curly, long or straight.

LIAM ON HIS STYLE:

"I like dressing simply. Just chucking on a pair of jeans and a T-shirt, and if I want to go all agricultural, I'll throw on a gilet."

SAY WHAT?!

The 1D boys say the funniest things...

HARRY

"Louis and I went swimming in our boxers one morning, then woke Niall up by flinging our dripping wet pants in his face.

ZAYN

"I don't have **smelly feet. I change my socks every day so they should smell reasonably well."**

NIALL

"Louis's feet smell the worst. Literally like **dog poo** on a stick – that bad!"

HARRY

Harry (on his 18th birthday): "I feel like I've woken up with suddenly more facial hair and a deeper voice."

"I don't care what any lad our age says, there's no way they've gone through their entire life without **wearing their boxer shorts two days in a row.**"

LOUIS

LIAM

Liam (on dressing like Louis): "Louis is a bit out there for me and I don't have the ankles for short trousers."

"I hate the pictures from the tour where we've got our arms in the air and we've got big sweat patches."

NIALL

LOUIS

If I was to fight anybody over anything, it would be with Niall for eating with his mouth open. It makes me feel sick.

LIAM

I used to practise snogging on the back of my hand. I'm not embarrassed, everybody's done it.

NIALL

"I'm still a bit of a scruff and I **fart** all the time."

ZAYN

When we're not together, we send each other messages saying, 'I really miss you'. I know that sounds really girlie, but that level of closeness is important.

LOUIS

"My little sister's friends are always getting me to sign posters. I think they must auction them off on the school bus."

HARRY

"We get into **trouble** about five times a day. We're not polished and well behaved."

NIALL

"The worst thing a girl could do on a date is fart louder than me."

BUMPER QUIZ

Think you know everything about the One Direction lads? Test your knowledge here...

1. What star sign is Louis?
2. How tall is Harry?
3. What is Zayn's favourite song on *Up All Night*?
4. Who is Niall's all time favourite musician?
5. Whose mum is called Karen?
6. Whose birthday is on Christmas Eve?
7. What is Niall's older brother called?
8. Which band member was born three weeks early?
9. Who has a Yin and Yang tattoo on their wrist?
10. Which 1D member has four sisters?
11. What is Harry's mum called?
12. What does Liam have a fear of?
13. What is Niall's favourite part of his own body?
14. Who is really fast at running?
15. On what date did 1D release *What Makes You Beautiful* in the US?
16. Which job did Louis's mum used to do that involves babies?
17. Who has a tattoo of a star?
18. Who would Zayn most like to duet with?
19. Who does Louis wish would follow him on Twitter?
20. Who prefers brunettes?
21. What was the first song that Harry knew all the words to?
22. Which boy prefers being in relationships to being single?
23. Who has appeared in Waterloo Road?
24. What food did Harry eat on his 18th birthday when he went out with his parents?
25. How many pairs of shoes do the boys have between them?
26. What kind of dog does Zayn have at home?
27. What does Harry sometimes do when he's sleeping?
28. What is Louis's favourite shoe brand?
29. Which member of the band likes wearing varsity jackets?
30. Who would like to meet a girl that he could take home to his parents?

GIRLS RULE!

Niall, Louis, Liam, Harry and Zayn have trillions of girls following them everywhere! But what kind of girl do they really like?

A sense of humour is key

All five of the boys like someone they can have a good laugh with. This isn't surprising when you think about the boys' legendary banter.

Harry also likes someone who's loyal and he really wants to be able to take a girl home to meet his parents.

Niall agrees that a good sense of humour is really important. He probably goes for brunettes more and likes nice eyes.

Zayn likes girls who are good at listening, and show that they are interested in him as a person. "If it looks like they've taken time out to come and speak to you, that's attractive," he says.

Liam likes girls who are a little shy. And he always notices if a girl has really nice eyes.

Celebrity crushes

Zayn's celeb crush is Megan Fox.
Louis would go for Katy Perry or Natalie Portman.
Liam likes Kim Kardashian.
Demi Lovato would be Niall's choice.
Alexa Chung is Harry's celeb crush.

Talking about feelings

Harry says he can get quite soppy when it comes to girls; especially when he really likes them.

Zayn reckons he's not very good at showing his emotions. "Maybe I'll change when I get older," he says.

Liam has never written a love letter. However, he's a great big softie when it comes to relationships. "If I dump a girl and then they cry, I'd instantly just get back with them," he says.

Louis thinks he will never understand girls, despite having four sisters!

Dating fans

All of the boys say they would happily date a fan. As Harry says, "If you like someone, you like someone." But it would have to be the right person. The boys all agree that personality is far more important than looks. A girl needs to be able to join in with banter and have a laugh. As Niall says, "If they haven't got a personality then the looks don't mean anything."

LOVE FACTS

- Niall's accent always makes girls swoon. He has no idea why.
- Zayn believes in love at first sight.
- The lads like to ask girls how they're doing on Twitter and make them laugh.
- Zayn prefers being in a relationship to being single.

OVER TO YOU!

One Direction really do love their fans. Along with the boys, we ran a competition for fans to ask anything they wanted. Here, the winners ask 1D what they really want to know.

NIALL

If you weren't in One Direction what would you be doing now?
OLIVIA CULLEN

"I'd be in my first year at university studying sound engineering. That's if I got into uni because I didn't get a chance to finish my exams. I'd still be singing and trying my best to get my name out there. I probably would have gone in for The X Factor again so who knows?"

If you could change one thing about your life what would it be?
EMILY NORRISH

"I'd like to go home more. I miss my friends and family and although it's great talking to them on the phone, it's not the same as seeing them. Skype is the best invention in the world though. I use it all the time."

If you could only have one thing in the world besides family and friends, what would it be and why?
LAURYN GUEST

"Music. Probably my guitar. I love taking my guitar around with me when we travel if I can, but it costs a fortune in excess baggage so I tend to leave it at home most of the time. If there's one around in a studio we're in, I'll have a go on that though."

LIAM

What's the strangest thing that's ever happened to you?
MOLLY 'ANN-MAY' MARRIOT

"It has to be when we hung out in the studio with Justin Bieber in America, and then went to his house. He's such a nice guy. I'd seen him do this rap on YouTube and I mentioned it to him and he started doing it in his living room with just me sat there. It was like having my own private Bieber show. I was buzzing."

Have you ever thought of leaving the band?
ANNA WOODING

"No, I've never seriously thought about it. You have down days when you're having a bad day, but you just get on with it. Sometimes we get so much attention that I want five minutes to myself to relax, and I do miss home too because we don't get back a lot. It's funny because you don't realise how much you miss somewhere until you're away from it. But the positives of being in the band hugely outweigh the negatives. We're so lucky to be in the position we're in and sometimes you have to take a step back from it and appreciate it."

If you could star in any movie what would it be?
STACY BLACK

"Batman: *The Dark Knight*. I love all of the Batman films and I couldn't wait for the next one to come out. I've become a real superhero nerd. Now I can afford things I've realised I love superheroes and I bought loads of caps with various ones on the other day."

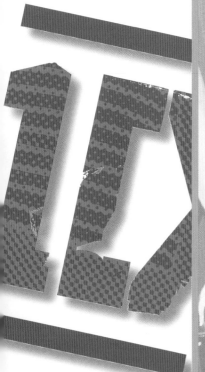

HARRY

I'm still too young to go on The X Factor, what advice would you give me to prepare?

EMMA NEWCOMBE

"Practise and practise as much as you can. Prepare and practise being as calm as you can be because nerves always show through, even though it's properly nerve-wracking. As long as you're prepared, things will be so much easier. And have fun."

Do you plan on making a movie? #hoping!

CHRISTINE LOUISE SUELTO QUINIVISTA

"We do have cameras with us a lot of the time so it would be great if we could make the footage into a movie."

Do you ever feel disappointed that you didn't make it as a solo artist or are you happy being in a band?

ERIN MCKENZIE

"I love being in a band with the other guys. I can't imagine being a solo artist now. It would be so weird. It would be odd travelling on your own and having no-one else on stage with you. We support each other and we're such good friends."

ZAYN

What is your favourite memory since One Direction started?

CHENICE GYNN

"Being on stage with Robbie Williams during The X Factor was sick. He was amazing and hung out with us all day. He was the most normal celeb ever and just sat chatting with us and invited us out to his winnebago. He's such a good guy. He's a born star."

Do you have any lucky items or rituals that you use to perform, if so what are they?

AMY CRAIG

"I've got a necklace that I got given by someone close to me which I wear every day and I feel that brings me good luck. I always brush my teeth before I go on stage, and we all huddle together and psych each other up before we perform as well."

If you knew today was your last day on earth, how would you spend it and why?

AMRIT OBHI

"I'd go home and spend the day with my mum, my dad, my aunties, my sisters and all of my friends. I'd want a really normal day from beginning to end and to spend it with the people I care about."

LOUIS

If you were a girl for a day what would you do and why?

ERIN HEATH

"I don't think I'd wear make-up because I don't like girls that wear a lot of make-up. And I definitely wouldn't wear heels because some girls look so ridiculous when they wear them and can't walk in them properly. But I would wear skin-tight jeans because you can get away with them when you're a girl."

What's your favourite way to relax away from all the stress?

LIZBETH MIRANDA

"I like having a bath, then lying in bed watching a good film. If I'm watching a film with my girlfriend I don't mind a rom-com, but if I'm on my own I like action movies that keep you on edge."

If you could change one thing about yourself what would it be?

JOYCE MUDZINGA

"I'd try and make myself tidier because I think it annoys people that I'm so messy. My hotel room is always an absolute tip and as stupid as it sounds, I always leave the sign on the door saying I don't want my room cleaned because I don't like the idea of someone moving my stuff about. Basically everything is everywhere and I always end up standing on a plug or something."

SSHHH! 18 AMAZING SECRETS ABOUT ONE DIRECTION!

1

Jennifer Aniston was Liam's first celebrity crush.

2

Niall went to an all-boys' school so isn't used to all this attention from girls.

3

Louis's favourite biscuit is a Crinkle Crunch or a chocolate Hob Nob.

4

Harry suffers from hay fever.

5

Zayn always wears two pairs of socks.

6

Niall uses Lynx deodorant.

7

Harry is a great cook. His speciality is Mexican food.

8

The boys do lots of charity work. They are all ambassadors for Rays of Sunshine – a charity that grants wishes for seriously ill children in the UK.

9

Harry wants to call his first daughter Darcey.

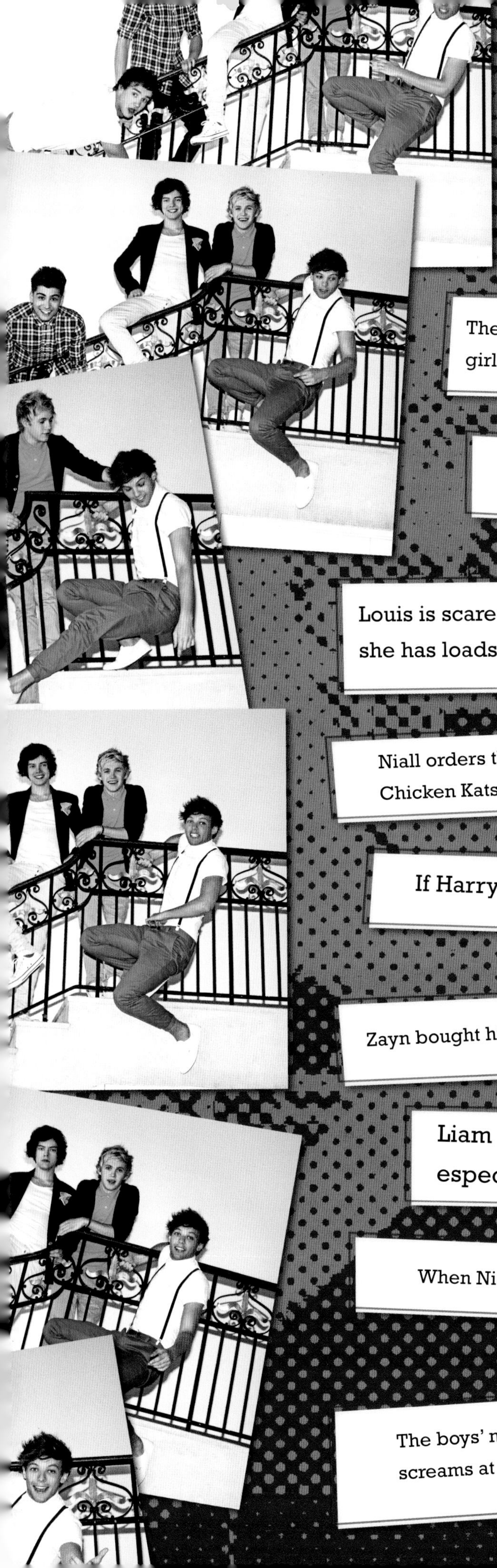

Thought you knew everything about the band? Think again...

The most romantic thing Louis has ever done is buy his girlfriend a ticket to LA because she was missing him. Aww.

10

Harry once ran through a train station in just his boxer shorts for a dare.

11

Louis is scared his little sister fancies Harry as she has loads of pictures of him on her Facebook page.

12

Niall orders the same meal every time he goes to Wagamama: Chicken Katsu Curry and crispy squid.

13

If Harry wasn't in 1D he'd like to be a physiotherapist.

14

Zayn bought his mum a Corsa car when she was learning to drive.

15

Liam doesn't like girls who wear too much fake tan, especially if they have orange hands.

16

When Niall is nervous he gets hyperactive.

17

The boys' managers have worked out that the crowd's screams at a 1D concert reach an ear-piercing 104 decibels.

18

BOY BAND BFFS

The boys are pretty much with each other 24/7, so it's no wonder they've become such great mates...

One Direction may be superstars, but the five boys are still keeping their feet very much on the ground. At heart they will always be five lads from normal backgrounds and they will never forget where they come from. "We're just five ordinary lads," laughs Niall. "It's unbelievable really."

As One Direction have discovered, fame and success come with a huge price tag. It might sound like a dream lifestyle – jetting all over the world, being adored by millions of people – but it can also be incredibly stressful. So it's no wonder the boys have come to rely so heavily on each other. As Louis says, "There's so much travelling involved. You'd get really lonely on your own. It's good that we have each other."

More importantly when so many young stars get caught up in the 'unreal' world of showbiz, the boys know they can trust each other to tell the truth – whether or not they want to hear it. "There's no way any of us would let each other get away with diva behaviour," says Liam. "They'd soon get a slap."

This close relationship between the boys is crucial, as life as international pop stars means they hardly get to see their family and friends.

This is something they find difficult to handle, as for One Direction home is very definitely where the heart is. "I miss just chilling out with friends and family and feeling a bit normal," says Zayn. "So it's good to have the lads to keep things real."

> **"There's no way any of us would let each other get away with diva behaviour. They'd soon get a slap."**

The lads not only work together, they're best mates too and this close friendship shines through wherever they go. They know they're lucky to have each other and make sure they keep each other's spirits up. They know exactly how to make each other feel better whenever they're feeling stressed or low. As Niall explains, "The lads are great if anyone is feeling down, they always get behind each other."

"Any day I need a cuddle I'll knock on Harry's door and give him a big hug," Louis adds. "The majority of the time I do go to Harry if I'm a bit down because I'm really close to him and we understand each other. Liam's also a great guy to comfort you."

Despite their huge fame, the boys have managed to stay as untarnished as they come. All five lads love their rare time out of the spotlight when they can watch movies, hang out with friends, watch TV or play computer games. Their heroes are still their mums and dads. As Louis explains, "I'll tell you what's really nice about all this experience that we never really bring up in interviews is the fact that we make our mums proud." One thing's for certain, their mums have every reason to be proud of them.

WHAT'S NEXT?

The boys have become very hot stars – selling millions of copies of their singles and albums all over the world. It may be hard to reach the top, but things don't get any easier once you're there. Having succeeded, the pressure is on to keep on succeeding. But there's no way that their flame will burn out as quickly as it ignited. As artists, they know they have to keep evolving and doing new things to keep themselves and their fans happy. They're always looking for the next step, they know they've got to keep pushing themselves forwards. They have enough talent and the right attitude to see them through. They approach everything they do with a happy, light-hearted attitude that is one hundred per cent contagious. As Harry says, "This is our job. We're doing what we're supposed to do. And if things go the way we want them to, we'll be doing this for the rest of our lives."

Not only do the boys have a sell-out world arena tour, their latest album is taking things to yet another level. It's one of the albums of the year and it's much, much more than just a follow-up to their debut, *Up All Night*. It still has that distinctive One Direction sound, but shows just how much the boys have grown as artists. They're that little bit wiser, far more confident and completely in control. As Liam explains, "Time, and performing to thousands of people, has given me confidence. We feel more confident as a group."

There is no doubt that this has been a phenomenal year for Harry, Zayn, Louis, Niall and Liam. But knowing the boys, we haven't seen anything yet. So what's next for 1D?

All five lads are justifiably proud of their album. As Niall says, "We're definitely older and wiser and that comes across in our music." And as Louis adds, "We believe if we keep on working hard, we'll continue to be successful."

Looking at what they've achieved, it's easy to forget just how young the boys are, and how far they've come in such a short time. The way it all exploded so quickly has left them amazed, grateful and more than a little bit dazed. More importantly, they've managed to keep their feet firmly on the ground and know they can't afford to relax if their success is to continue.

"It's humbling," says Harry. "We're just five normal boys who have been given this opportunity."

"It's incredible," adds Liam, "I don't think we could ever have imagined anything like this. It's beyond our wildest dreams."

Harry, Louis, Zayn, Liam and Niall have become part of our everyday world – a sign of true celebrity. They've made the kind of start that has labelled them a worldwide pop phenomenon. On top of the extraordinary record sales they've managed to achieve in such a short time, One Direction have become pop icons to millions of fans around the world. They've taken the world by storm and left it begging for more. We can't wait to see what's next on their incredible journey. And one thing's for sure, they'll be sharing it with the people who are the most important to them – their fans.

A MESSAGE FROM ONE DIRECTION

As ever, the boys know they owe it all to you, the fans, so here's a last word from them to you...

ZAYN: "A massive thank you for all the support and dedication and the times you wait outside in the cold to buy tickets to come and see us, or buy our album. There would be no One Direction without the fans and we're so grateful that you've been there every step of the way."

LOUIS: "A massive, massive thank you. We owe every single bit of our success to you. The fans are the ones who voted for us in The X Factor and gave us the platform to try our luck in the rest of the world. They spread the word on Twitter and got our name out there and we're so grateful."

LIAM: "Thank you so much for making this whole thing so incredible and bigger than we could ever have imagined. We can't believe that One Direction are global now. We were just young lads coming out of a TV show and now people around the world know our names. It's so strange when people know everything about you. For instance, when we went to Australia for the first time, even though no-one knew us they knew everything about us. And it's all thanks to you guys, so thank you."

NIALL: "I'd like to say thank you to every single person out there who has supported us since day one. And I'd also like to welcome new fans to the One Direction family. Thank you for helping our album do so well and hopefully the next year will be just as much fun."

HARRY: "A massive, massive thank you. We just can't thank you enough, honestly. You've put us where we are and we wouldn't be here without you. We will be forever grateful."